Cracking MATHS

2nd Class

Practice Book

Majella O'Connor, Aishling Doyle, Joan Gilligan,
Carmel Kelly, Catherine Knight

g GILL EDUCATION

Gill Education
Hume Avenue
Park West
Dublin 12
www.gilleducation.ie

Gill Education is an imprint of M. H. Gill & Co.

ISBN: 978 07171 54203

© Majella O'Connor, Aishling Doyle, Joan Gilligan, Carmel Kelly, Catherine Knight 2014

Design: Design Image
Print origination: Carole Lynch
Internal illustrations: Kate Shannon
Technical drawings: MPS Limited
Cover illustration: www.designbos.ie
Consultant editor in mathematics curriculum and pedagogy: Betty Stoutt

The paper used in this book comes from the wood pulp of sustainably managed forests.

For permission to reproduce photographs, the authors and publisher gratefully acknowledge the following:

© Alamy: 7, 42TR, 42BL; © Shutterstock: 10, 26, 39, 40, 42TL, 42BC, 42BR, 55, 58, 59.

The authors and publisher have made every effort to trace all copyright holders, but if any has been inadvertently
overlooked we would be pleased to make the necessary arrangement at the first opportunity.

Contents

Doubles and Near Doubles

1. 1 + 1 = ☐   5 + 5 = ☐   2 + 2 = ☐   6 + 6 = ☐

   3 + 3 = ☐   4 + 4 = ☐   8 + 8 = ☐   5 + 6 = ☐

   9 + 9 = ☐   7 + 7 = ☐   1 + 2 = ☐   6 + 5 = ☐

   2 + 3 = ☐   6 + 7 = ☐   3 + 4 = ☐   9 + 10 = ☐

   8 + 9 = ☐   7 + 8 = ☐   4 + 5 = ☐   10 + 11 = ☐

   1 + 0 = ☐   5 + 4 = ☐   2 + 1 = ☐   10 + 10 = ☐

   3 + 2 = ☐   4 + 3 = ☐   8 + 7 = ☐   10 + 9 = ☐

2.
| 5 | 7 | 9 | 4 | 8 | 6 | 2 | 1 | 10 | 3 |
| +6 | +8 | +10 | +5 | +9 | +7 | +3 | +2 | +10 | +4 |

3.
| 5 | 7 | 9 | 4 | 8 | 6 | 2 | 1 | 10 | 3 |
| +4 | +6 | +8 | +3 | +7 | +5 | +1 | +0 | +9 | +2 |

4. Tess and Lucy were skipping. Tess made 3 more jumps than Lucy.

There is one possibility in the table.

Can you write some more?

Tess might have made ___ jumps.	Lucy might have made ___ jumps.
10	7

Mental Maths 1

1. 3 tens 4 units = ☐

2. 30c = 10c + ☐ + ☐ + ☐

3. 10 more than 50 = ☐

4. Mia had 20c. She spent 12c on a copy.
   How much had she left? ☐

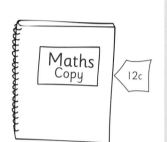

5. A cube has ☐ faces.

6. Put these numbers in
   order, starting with the lowest: 32, 47, 74, 23, 11

   ☐ ☐ ☐ ☐ ☐

7. Circle the even numbers.

   17   12   8   13   14

8. 67 = ☐ tens ☐ units

9. 11, 13, 15, ☐ , ☐

10. Show half past 4 on the clock.

Score

Mental Maths 2

1. $90 =$ ⬚ tens.

2. Jack had 20c. He bought an orange for 13c. How much had he left? ⬚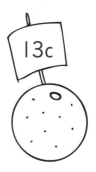

3. If today is Wednesday, what day was it yesterday? ⬚

4. True or false? $17 > 9 + 5$ ⬚

5.

t   u

⬚

6. Fiona is 3 years older than Joseph. Joseph is 10 years old. How old is Fiona? ⬚

7. $20c = $ ◯ $+$ ◯

8. $\frac{1}{2}$ of $20 =$ ⬚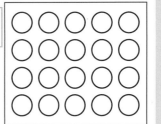

9. 16 is double ⬚

10. Put these numbers in order, starting with the biggest.

49	73	11	65	89	7
⬚	⬚	⬚	⬚	⬚	⬚

Score

This is a block graph of the children's favourite characters.

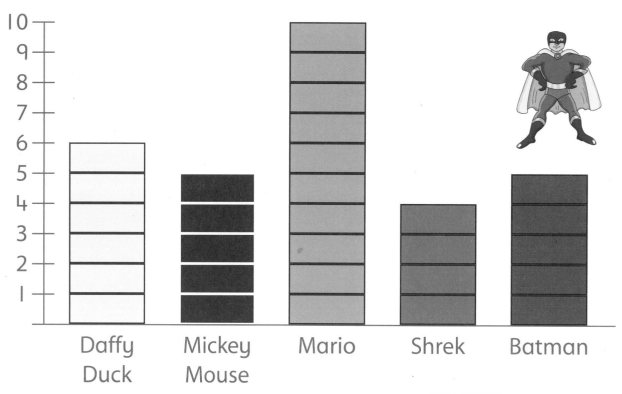

1. How many children like Mickey Mouse? ☐

2. How many children like Shrek? ☐

3. Which is the most popular character? ☐

4. Which is the least popular character? ☐

5. How many children altogether like Mario and Batman? ☐

6. How many more children prefer Mario to Mickey Mouse? ☐

7. How many fewer children prefer Shrek to Daffy Duck? ☐

8. How many children altogether like Daffy Duck, Mickey Mouse and Mario? ☐

9. Which character is as popular as Mickey Mouse?

☐

10. How many children altogether are there in the class? ☐

Test Yourself!   Data

Ms O'Shea had 5 DVDs. The children in second class voted to see which film they would watch. Here are the results of the vote.

- Finding Nemo 3
- Ice Age 6
- Madagascar 7
- Toy Story 5
- Cars 5

1. Fill in the block graph. Colour one block for every child. Use a different colour for each film.

7					
6					
5					
4					
3					
2					
1					
	Finding Nemo	Ice Age	Cars	Madagascar	Toy Story

2. Which was the most popular film?

3. Which was the second most popular film?

4. Which was the least popular film?

5. How many children altogether wanted to watch **Cars** and **Ice Age**?

6. How many children are in the class?

7. How many more children preferred **Madagascar** to **Toy Story**?

8. How many fewer children preferred **Cars** to **Ice Age**?

9. Which film was as popular as **Cars**?

10. How many children altogether liked **Cars**, **Finding Nemo** and **Madagascar**?

Mental Maths 3

1. $5 + 5 + 5 + 5 = 10 +$ ☐

2. $\frac{1}{2}$ of $16 =$ ☐

3.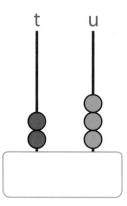

4. $70 -$ ☐ $= 50$

5. How many squares are there? ☐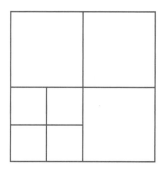

6. A tennis ball costs 5c. How many can I buy for 20c? ☐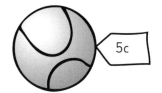

7. $26c =$ ◯ $c +$ ◯ $c +$ ◯ c

8. 32 units = ☐ tens ☐ units

9. $7 + 8 + 4 =$ ☐

10. $\frac{1}{2}$ of $18 =$ ☐

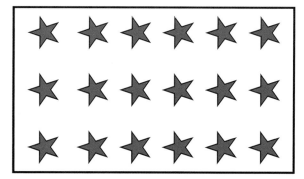

Score

Help the rabbit get to its burrow.

Add and then colour the squares where the answer has 7 units.

	t u 1 4 +2 3 ------ 3 7	t u 3 6 +2 3	t u 4 5 +1 7	t u 2 5 +2 6	t u 1 7 +5 4	t u 6 3 +2 8
t u 4 9 +2 5	t u 5 3 +2 4	t u 1 1 +3 6	t u 4 7 +1 0	t u 6 2 +1 5	t u 3 4 +1 3	t u 7 6 + 8
t u 3 9 +3 6	t u 4 9 +2 9	t u 2 5 +5 9	t u 1 7 +7 7	t u 4 8 +3 5	t u 1 5 +6 2	t u 4 4 +1 9
t u 3 5 +4 3	t u 1 9 +2 7	t u 1 5 +3 8	t u 3 5 +1 5	t u 6 2 +1 7	t u 8 3 +1 4	t u 6 8 +2 1
t u 1 8 +1 8	t u 4 6 +2 6	t u 3 0 +3 8	t u 2 6 +1 9	t u 5 8 +2 7	t u 1 9 +5 8	t u 2 4 +3 5
t u 5 6 3 + 9	t u 4 2 6 + 5	t u 2 2 7 +3 7	t u 2 6 2 0 + 7	t u 2 1 +2 4	t u 3 6 2 3 +1 8	

Mental Maths 4

1. How many triangles? ☐

2. Finish the pattern.

   11, 22, 33, 44, ☐ , ☐

3. How much do I have?  ☐ c

4. Colour half of this shape.

5. 50c = ◯ c, ◯ c, ◯ c

6. 12 + ☐ = 30

7. George had 40c. He gave $\frac{1}{2}$ of his money to his sister.
   How much had he left? ☐

8. Each team has 6 players. How many players are on
   4 teams? ☐

9. 16 and 20 have a difference of 4.
   What is the difference between 2 and 13? ☐

10. Put these times in order, starting with the earliest.

    4 o'clock $\frac{1}{2}$ past 2   5 o'clock $\frac{1}{2}$ past 3

    ☐ , ☐ , ☐ , ☐

Score

1. Draw shapes in the boxes below. Name the shape.

a) A shape with 1 curved side

b) A shape with 4 straight sides.

c) A shape with 3 sides.

d) A shape with 2 sides.

2. What shapes can you see? Choose the right words from the word box.

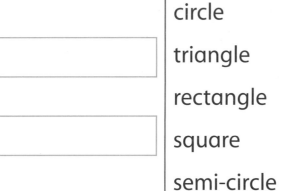

Word Box
circle
triangle
rectangle
square
semi-circle
oval

3. a) Two semi-circles make a [   ]

   b) If I cut a square in half I could get a [   ] or a [   ]

   c) If I cut a rectangle in quarters I could get a

   [   ] , a [   ] or a [   ]

What shapes can you see? (Ring) the correct words.

1.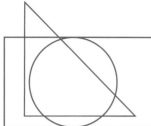

    square   circle   rectangle

    oval   triangle   semi-circle

2.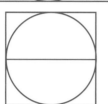

    square   circle   rectangle

    oval   triangle   semi-circle

3.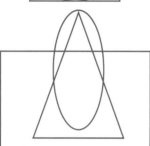

    square   circle   rectangle

    oval   triangle   semi-circle

True ✓ or false ✗ ?

4. This is a circle.

5.  A rectangle has 4 equal sides.

6.  This is a semi-circle.

7. A triangle has 3 corners.

8. An oval has 1 curved side.

9. 2 semi-circles make a circle.

10. How many triangles?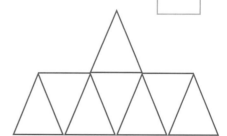

Mental Maths 5

1. Show $\frac{1}{2}$ past 5 on this clock.

2. Jenny is 127cm tall.
   Tom is 9cm taller
   than her. How tall is Tom?

   [ ] cm

3. Which of these 3-D shapes can roll?

   cone   cube   cuboid   [   ]

4. Draw the line of symmetry in this shape.

5. $12 + 16 = 10 +$ [ ]

6. $25 +$ [ ] $= 40$

7. 1 ten and 15 units
   = [ ] tens and 5 units

8. Which is heavier, the apple
   or the banana ? [   ]

9. $47 - 25 =$ [ ]

10. $\frac{1}{2}$ of $26 =$ [ ]

Score

1. How many right angles in each shape?

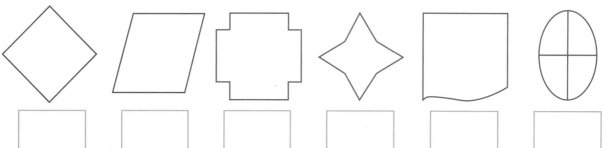

2.

| Draw this right angle after a $\frac{1}{2}$ rotation. | Draw this right angle after a $\frac{1}{4}$ rotation to the left. | Hints |

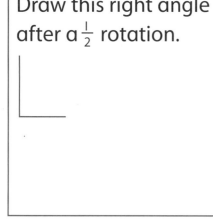
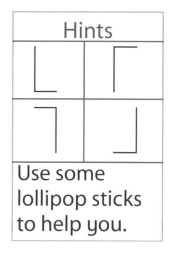

Use some lollipop sticks to help you.

3. Can you follow the clues to find the names of the children?

a) Start at K.

Make a half turn.

From this letter make a quarter turn to the left.

Make another half turn.

The girl's name is

b) Start at A.

Make a quarter rotation to the left.

From this letter make a half rotation to the right.

Now make a quarter turn to the left.

The boy's name is

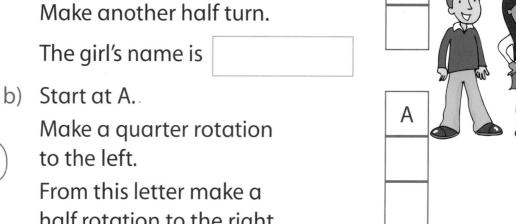

Mental Maths 6

1. Insert the correct sign   < or > or =

   13 + 9 ⬚ 28 − 6

2. What day is 2 days after Wednesday? ⬚

3. Finish this pattern.

   S,   M,   T,   W, ⬚ , ⬚ , S

4. Put these numbers in order, starting with the smallest.

   78   59   44   52   25   36   17

   ⬚ , ⬚ , ⬚ , ⬚ , ⬚ , ⬚ , ⬚

5. Show 67 on this abacus.

   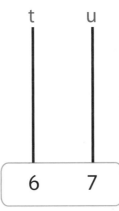

6. Show half past 8 on this clock.

   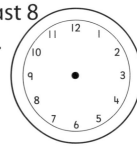

7. Aishling and Catherine shared 24 sweets equally between them. How many did each girl get? ⬚

8. 17 − ⬚ = 11

9. Circle the odd numbers.

   11   22   33   44   55

10. Grace had 31c. She bought a hairbrush for 11c. How much had she left? ⬚

Score

1	2	3	4	5	6	7	8	9	10	11	12	13	14	15	16	17	18	19	20

1. $8 - 3 = \boxed{}$ $\quad$ $11 - 5 = \boxed{}$ $\quad$ $17 - 7 = \boxed{}$ $\quad$ $13 - 5 = \boxed{}$

2. $6 - \boxed{} = 2$ $\quad$ $10 - \boxed{} = 9$ $\quad$ $12 - \boxed{} = 7$ $\quad$ $14 - \boxed{} = 8$

3.
t u	t u	t u	t u	t u	t u
3 7	7 3	5 3	5 3	2 8	4 8
− 1 5	− 5 2	− 3 2	− 4 1	− 1 1	− 2 7

4.
t u	t u	t u	t u	t u	t u
7 9	6 8	6 4	3 8	5 7	6 9
− 5 3	− 4 6	− 1 3	− 2 7	− 4 1	− 4 0

5.
t u	t u	t u	t u	t u	t u
5 7	7 6	9 4	7 4	9 5	8 7
− 1 5	− 5 3	− 8 1	− 6 2	− 7 3	− 3 6

6. $47 - 21 = \boxed{}$ $\quad$ $28 - 10 = \boxed{}$ $\quad$ $66 - 45 = \boxed{}$

$46 - 35 = \boxed{}$ $\quad$ $57 - 12 = \boxed{}$ $\quad$ $96 - 74 = \boxed{}$

7. Jack had 19 football cards. He lost 5. How many cards has Jack now? $\boxed{}$

8. Mary bought 37 sweets. She gave 16 to her sister. How many has she left? $\boxed{}$

9.
−	20	19	18
1			
2			

10.
−	35	37	39
2			
4			

Mental Maths 7

1. Write the missing number.

   [ ] , 60, 61, 62, 63, 64

2. Jack bought 2 bars of chocolate for 32c each. How much did he spend? [ ]

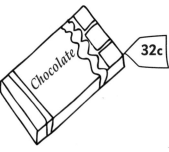

3. Isaac bought 18 sweets. He gave half of them to his brother. How many had he left ? [ ]

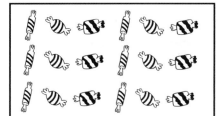

4. Colour the coins I need to make 50c.

5. $12 +$ [ ] $= 34$

6. 7 tens 5 units = [ ]

7. Colour $\frac{1}{2}$ of this set. ⟶

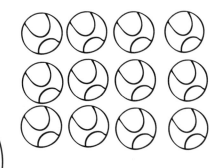

8. Show $\frac{1}{2}$ past 5 on this clock.

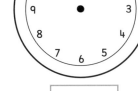

9. 10 more than 40 is [ ]

10. I have 25c. How many 5c lollipops can I buy? [ ]

Score

Practise!

Months of the Year

Time 1

> Thirty days hath September,
> April, June and November,
> All the rest have thirty-one,
> except for February alone,
> which has twenty-eight rain or shine,
> but in a leap year, twenty-nine.

Months		Number of days
January	$10 + 10 + 10 + 1 =$	
February	$20 + 8 =$	
	$20 + 4 + 5 =$	
March	$15 + 10 + 6 =$	
April	$40 - 10 =$	
May	$(20 + 20) - 9 =$	
June	$50 - 20 =$	
July	1 less than 32 $=$	
August	4 more than 27 $=$	
September	3 tens $=$	
October	3 tens and 1 unit $=$	
November	29 rounds to:	
December	$25 + 5 + 1 =$	

1. There are ☐ months in a year.

2. The first month is ☐

3. The seventh month is ☐

4. My birthday is in ☐

5. Which month comes before November? ☐

6. Which month usually has 28 days? ☐

7. New Year's Day is the first day of this month. ☐

8. In ☐ we put up our Christmas tree.

Group Work Make a block graph of birthdays in the class.

Mental Maths 8

1. Colour the shapes that can roll.

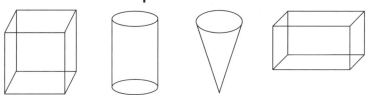

2. Put these numbers in order, starting with the smallest.

13   7   26   8   41

[   ] , [   ] , [   ] , [   ] , [   ]

3. What is the smallest numeral you can make from these numbers?   2   0   9   [   ]

4. How many $\frac{1}{2}$ litres are in 1 litre? [   ]

$\frac{1}{2}$ litre   1 litre

5. How many faces does a cube have? [   ]

6. Colour the 3rd shape after the number.

A,   M, 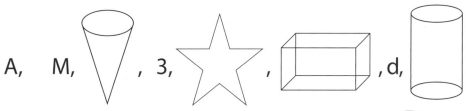 , 3, ⭐ , ▭ , d,

7. I have 36c. I want to buy a ball. How much more do I need? [   ]

50c

8. Show half past 7 on this digital clock. [:   ]

9. 3 dogs have [   ] legs.

10. 20 less than 70 is [   ]

Score
[   ]

1. Use lollipop sticks to measure the following.

   The length of the desk = [   ] lollipop sticks

   The width of my copy = [   ] lollipop sticks.

   The width of the window = [   ] lollipop sticks.

   The length of the book shelf = [   ] lollipop sticks.

2. Using your metre strip, find and draw an object that is less than a metre, more than a metre and about a metre in length.

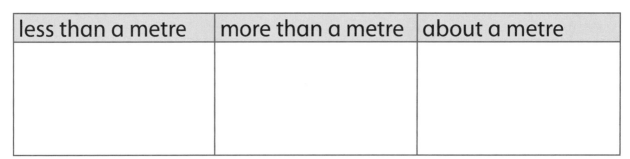

less than a metre	more than a metre	about a metre

3. True ✓ or false ✗ ?

   a) The width of my desk is longer than $\frac{1}{2}$ m. [   ]

   b) The length of 2 maths books is about the same as $\frac{1}{2}$ m. [   ]

   c) The height of the classroom door is shorter than $\frac{1}{4}$ m. [   ]

   d) The length of the book shelf is longer than $\frac{1}{2}$ m. [   ]

   e) The width of the whiteboard is about the same as $\frac{1}{4}$ m. [   ]

4. Draw lines to match these measurements. Start at the dot.

   a) 5cm   •

   b) 3cm   •

   c) 8cm   •

Test Yourself! Length

1. I metre = [ ] cm   2. $\frac{1}{2}$ m = [ ] cm

3. If you cut 1 metre of string in half, each piece will be [ ] m long.

4. How many $\frac{1}{4}$ m equal 1m? [ ]

5. A stack of books is 15cm high. Another stack of books is 12cm high. What is the total height of the 2 stacks of books? [ ] cm

6.
Mary	Jack	Jessica	Max

 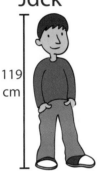 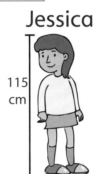 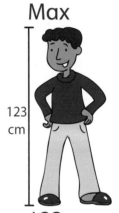

121 cm   119 cm   115 cm   123 cm

121cm   119cm   115cm   123cm

Who is the tallest? [ ] Who is the shortest? [ ]

7. The kitchen is 10m long. The dining room is 12m long. What is the difference between the length of the two rooms? [ ] cm

8. What is the total length of the two bricks? [ ]

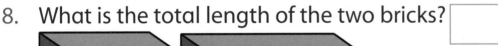

29 cm   38 cm

9. Measure these objects.

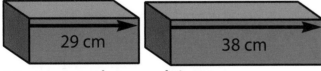 [ ]

 [ ]

10. Simon makes a train with blocks. It is 10cm long. He makes it 4cm longer. Then he take away half of the train. How long is the train now? [ ] cm

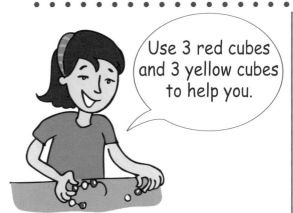

Use 3 red cubes and 3 yellow cubes to help you.

Lisa wants to make a bracelet for her friend. She has 6 beads. 3 are red and 3 are yellow.
Show 4 ways she can put the beads together.
Remember – each pattern must be different.

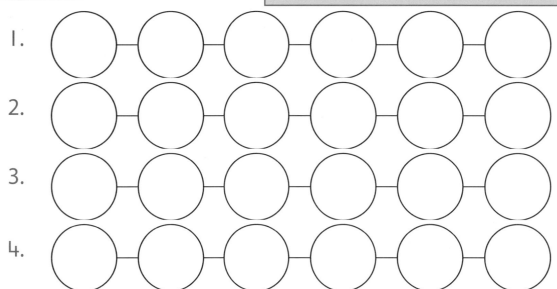

1.

2.

3.

4.

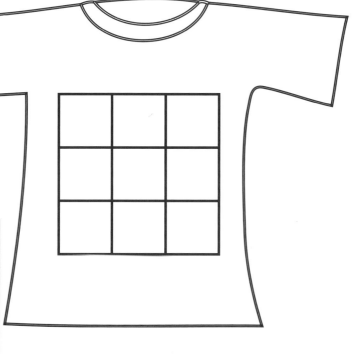

Leo has three fabric paints – blue, green and orange.
He wants to decorate his t-shirt so that each colour only appears once in each row and column. Can you help him?

Mental Maths 9

1. How many 10c coins are needed to make €1? ☐

2. Show quarter to 6 on this clock.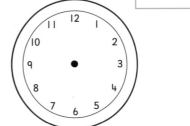

3. This pencil is ☐ cm long.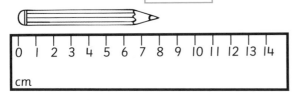

4. How many months have 30 days? ☐

5. Jack has 24 sweets. His sister Ella has twice as many as Jack. How many does Ella have? ☐

6. How many faces on a cylinder? ☐

7. Colour in $\frac{1}{4}$ of this pizza.

8. Put in the correct sign,
    <   or   >   or   =
    $3 + 7$ ☐ $4 + 6$

9. The total height of these two plants is ☐ cm.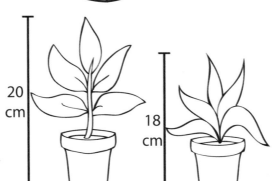

10. Write the missing coin.

$= €1$

Score ☐

Comparing and Ordering

1. Write the correct sign in each box.

greater than >	same as =	less than <

10 ☐ 20	32 ☐ 19	16 ☐ 16	24 ☐ 21
25 ☐ 36	18 ☐ 43	14 ☐ 31	19 ☐ 15
43 ☐ 47	26 ☐ 25	30 ☐ 13	20 ☐ 20
33 ☐ 3	57 ☐ 75	11 ☐ 22	35 ☐ 53

2. Write the correct sign.

6 + 9 ☐ 15 + 3	20 – 3 ☐ 14 + 4	14 – 2 ☐ 16 + 1
9 + 5 ☐ 11 + 3	50 – 20 ☐ 20 + 10	2 + 16 ☐ 11 + 9
27 – 10 ☐ 10 + 7	13 + 13 ☐ 20 + 7	50 – 10 ☐ 48 – 8
7 + 6 ☐ 15 – 5	8 + 8 ☐ 18 – 2	9 + 5 ☐ 7 + 7

3. Place these numbers in order from smallest to largest.

52   46   81   33   15   ☐ ☐ ☐ ☐ ☐

13   50   6   67   29   ☐ ☐ ☐ ☐ ☐

4. Find the words!

p	r	a	c	t	i	c	e
1st	2nd	3rd	4th	5th	6th	7th	last

2nd letter	3rd letter	5th letter

5th letter	3rd letter	1st letter

2nd letter	6th letter	7th letter	last letter

2nd letter	3rd letter	4th letter	last letter

Test Yourself!   Comparing and Ordering

Write the correct sign in each box < or > or =

1. a)   8 ☐ 8   13 ☐ 19   19 ☐ 20

    b)   14 ☐ 41   23 ☐ 26   47 ☐ 44

2. a)   12 ☐ 22   55 ☐ 35   76 ☐ 67

    b)   12 ☐ 11   50 ☐ 5   10 ☐ 10

Now try these.

3.   7 + 7 ☐ 15   13 – 8 ☐ 5

4.   9 + 7 ☐ 12   24 + 6 ☐ 27

5.   6 + 9 ☐ 15 + 0   11 – 3 ☐ 14 + 4

6.   14 – 2 ☐ 16 + 1   20 + 5 ☐ 11 + 9

7.   5 – 2 ☐ 2 + 10   6 + 6 ☐ 11 – 3

8. Place these numbers in order, from largest to smallest.

    28   35   21   17   50   ☐ ☐ ☐ ☐ ☐

9. Place these numbers in order, from smallest to largest.

    92   34   19   56   43   ☐ ☐ ☐ ☐ ☐

10. True ✓ or false ✗ ?

    17 > 19   ☐   16 = 8 + 8   ☐

    16 – 3 < 14 – 2 ☐   9 + 9 > 20 – 4   ☐

Mental Maths 10

1. 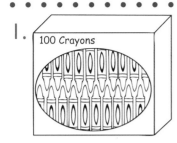 + 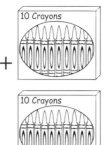 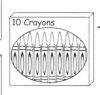 +  = [ ] crayons

2. How much money do I have? [ ]

3. A cuboid has [ ] corners.

4. Colour the longer scarf.

5. Colour the seventh kite yellow.

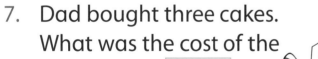

6. Draw two lines of symmetry in this shape. [ ]

7. Dad bought three cakes. What was the cost of the three cakes? [ ]

8. What time is it? [ ]

9. Half of 40 is [ ]

10. What is the difference between 21 and 9? [ ]

Score

1. Use the squares to complete the patterns below.
   Complete and colour the symmetrical patterns.

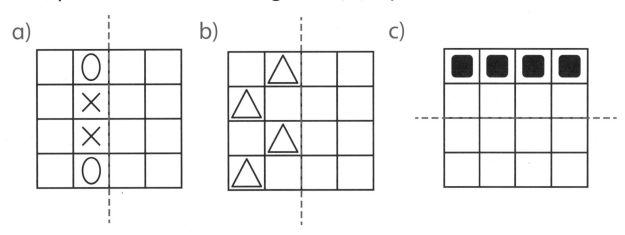

a)   b)   c)

2. Find 4 symmetrical and 4 non-symmetrical pictures below.
   Place the words in the correct box underneath.

| television | Eiffel Tower | snowman | tree | fish |
| mask | banana | clothes hanger | desk | pumpkin |

symmetrical ✔		non-symmetrical ✘	

True ✓ or false ✗ ?

1. This angle is a right angle.
 ☐

2. This angle is smaller than a right angle.
 ☐

3. This angle is bigger than a right angle.
 ☐

4. A butterfly has one line of symmetry.
 ☐

5. This shape has 6 right angles.
 ☐

6. A square corner is known as a right angle. ☐

7. This letter has no right angles.
 ☐

8. A square has 5 right angles. ☐

9. A semi-circle has one line of symmetry.
 ☐

10 Ring the symmetrical letter.

R   J   M

Mental Maths 11

1. How many $\frac{1}{2}$ litre cartons of apple juice do I need to make 2 litres? ☐

2. How many months have 31 days? ☐

3. Show 1:30 on this clock.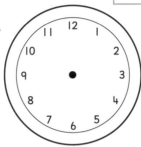

4. Name a 3-D shape that cannot roll. ☐

5. Draw the fewest coins to make €1.50.

6. What time is it?

☐

7. What is the sum of 12, 13 and 14? ☐

8. March and April are in the season of ☐

9. Colour the heavier fruit.

10.

10			
9			
8			
7			
6			
5			
4			
3			
2			
1			
apples	oranges	bananas	pears

☐ more children prefer apples to bananas.

Score ☐

1. Use cubes and a balance. Estimate, weigh and record.

object	estimate	measurement in cubes
library book		
5 crayons		
glue stick		
paint brush		

2. Using a bag of sugar and a balance, find and draw two objects that are lighter than a kilogram.

3. Draw two objects that are heavier than 1 kilogram.

4. True ✓ or false ✗?

   a) The duster is heavier than $\frac{1}{2}$ kg. ☐

   b) The whiteboard marker is lighter than $\frac{1}{4}$ kg. ☐

   c) My homework notebook weighs about $\frac{1}{2}$ kg. ☐

   d) My pencil case is heavier than $\frac{1}{4}$ kg. ☐

   e) My lunch box is about the same as $\frac{1}{2}$ kg. ☐

   f) My shoe is heavier than $\frac{1}{4}$ kg. ☐

1. Which would take more cubes to balance it?

   A pencil or your maths book? [_____]

2. If you had to balance an apple, which measuring unit would you use – lollipop sticks or lunch boxes?

   [_____]

3. Put these weights in order, starting with the lightest.

   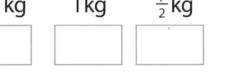

   2kg $\frac{1}{4}$ kg   1 kg $\frac{1}{2}$ kg

   [____] [____] [____] [____]

4. Name two things lighter than 1 kg.

   [_____] [_____]

5. Name two things heavier than 1 kg.

   [_____] [_____]

6. How many $\frac{1}{2}$ kg do you need to make one kilogram? [____]

7. Can you name one thing lighter than $\frac{1}{4}$ kg? [____]

8. How many $\frac{1}{4}$ kg do you need to make one kilogram? [____]

9. A bag of potatoes weighs 5kg.
   How heavy are 6 bags of potatoes? [____] kg

   Potatoes
   5kg

10. A farmer has a vegetable stall in a market.
    He has 20kg of carrots. He sells 6kg in the morning and 8kg in the afternoon.
    How many kilograms
    has he left? [____] kg

Mental Maths 12

1. Write the price of the pencil using the euro sign. [ ]

   29c

2. Circle the heavier box of fruit.

   ½ kg   ¼ kg

3. What number is this?

h	t	u
		○
		○
		○
		○
		○
		○
	●	○
	●	○
○	●	○

   [ ]

4. Two days after Tuesday is [ ]

5. Colour the coins you need to make €1.15.

6. Ann's scarf is [ ] cm longer than Sue's scarf.

   Sue's scarf is 32cm

   Ann's scarf is 39cm

7. Joseph has 10 marbles. John has twice as many marbles as Joseph. How many have they altogether? [ ]

8. A farmer had 94 goats. He sold 7 of them. How many had he left? [ ]

9. Write the missing number.

   177, 178, 179, [ ]

10. The sum of 16 and 18 is [ ]

Score

> ... when the long hand is at 12, it says o'clock
>
> when the long hand is at 6, it is $\frac{1}{2}$ past
>
> when the long hand is at 3, it is $\frac{1}{4}$ past
>
> when the long hand is at 9, it is $\frac{1}{4}$ to

1. Tell your friend how to make the clock say these times.

   4 o'clock   11 o'clock $\frac{1}{2}$ past 7 $\frac{1}{2}$ past 9

   $\frac{1}{4}$ past 2 $\frac{1}{4}$ past 12 $\frac{1}{4}$ to 5 $\frac{1}{4}$ to 4

2. Draw the long and short hands.

   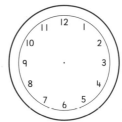 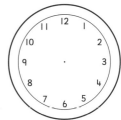

6 o'clock $\frac{1}{2}$ past 2 $\frac{1}{4}$ past 8 $\frac{1}{4}$ past 1 $\frac{1}{2}$ past 12

   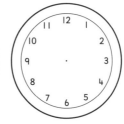 

$\frac{1}{4}$ to 5 $\frac{1}{4}$ to 6 $\frac{1}{4}$ past 6 $\frac{1}{4}$ past 10 $\frac{1}{4}$ past 7

3.   1 hour earlier   1 hour later

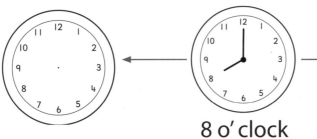

8 o' clock

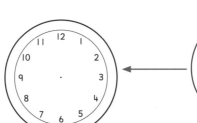 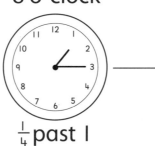

$\frac{1}{4}$ past 1

True ✓ or false ✗ ?

1. There are nine days in a week.

2. 14 days make a fortnight.

3. There are 12 months in a year.

4. May, June and July are the months of summer.

5. There are 31 days in June.

6. There are 24 hours in one day.

7. There are 15 minutes in $\frac{1}{2}$ an hour.

8. What time is it?

9. Make the clock say:

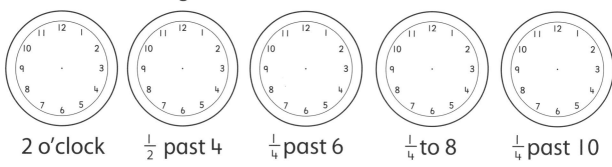

2 o'clock $\frac{1}{2}$ past 4 $\frac{1}{4}$ past 6 $\frac{1}{4}$ to 8 $\frac{1}{4}$ past 10

10. Match the time to the digital clocks.

$\frac{1}{2}$ past 9   1 o'clock $\frac{1}{2}$ past 5 $\frac{1}{2}$ past 7 $\frac{1}{2}$ past 11   2 o'clock

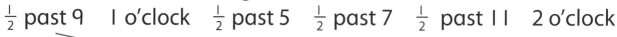

1:00	5:30	9:30	2:00	11:30	7:30

Mental Maths 13

1. Joe has 17 toy cars. Pat has 30 more cars than Joe. How many cars have they between them?

2. Colour the object that has the smaller surface area.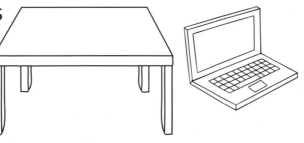

3. There were 40 daffodils in the garden. Mammy picked 8 of them. How many are left?

4. Jane had 16 sweets. She gave half of her sweets to Tim. How many had she left?

5. Is this shape:

   a) a circle?   b) an oval?   c) a triangle?

6. What number is shown on this abacus?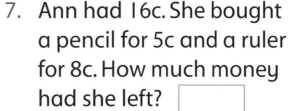

7. Ann had 16c. She bought a pencil for 5c and a ruler for 8c. How much money had she left?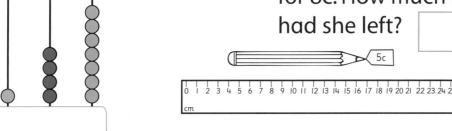

8. How many legs do 4 cats have altogether?

9. 17 + ☐ = 25

10. Fill in the missing numerals from the 100-square.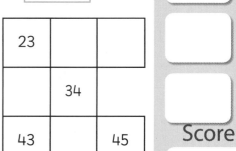

23		
	34	
43		45

Score

1. Colour in steps of 2.

| 1 | 2 | 3 | 4 | 5 | 6 | 7 | 8 | 9 | 10 |
| 11 | 12 | 13 | 14 | 15 | 16 | 17 | 18 | 19 | 20 |

2. Fill in the missing numbers.

3,   6,   ☐ , ☐ , ☐ , ☐ , ☐ , ☐ , ☐ , ☐

3. Count in 4s.

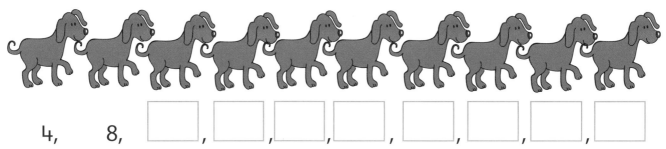

4,   8,   ☐ , ☐ , ☐ , ☐ , ☐ , ☐ , ☐ , ☐

4. Colour in steps of 5.

1	2	3	4	5	6	7	8	9	10
11	12	13	14	15	16	17	18	19	20
21	22	23	24	25	26	27	28	29	30
31	32	33	34	35	36	37	38	39	40
41	42	43	44	45	46	47	48	49	50

5. Fill in the missing numbers.

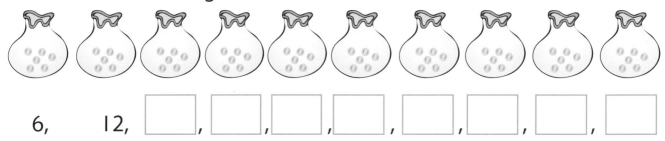

6,   12,   ☐ , ☐ , ☐ , ☐ , ☐ , ☐ , ☐

Continue the patterns …

1. | 2 | | 6 | | | 14 | | | 20 |

2. | 3 | 6 | 9 | | | | | | |

3. | 4 | | 16 | | | | | | |

4. | 5 | | 20 | | | | | | |

5. | 6 | | | 30 | | 48 | | |

6. | 10 | 20 | | 50 | | | | |

7. How many fingers?

   a) 3 children [ ]   b) 5 children [ ]

   c) 8 children [ ]

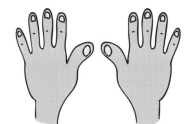

8. How many wheels?

   a) 4 tricycles [ ]   b) 6 tricycles [ ]

   c) 10 tricycles [ ]

9. How many legs?

   a) 2 sheep [ ]   b) 5 sheep [ ]

   c) 9 sheep [ ]

10. How many eggs?

    a) 3 boxes [ ]   b) 2 boxes [ ]

    c) 5 boxes [ ]

Mental Maths 14

1. Tom has 12 football cards. James has 10 more than that.
    How many cards does James have? ⬚

2. Colour $\frac{1}{4}$ of these bananas.

3. What comes next? | 4 | 8 | 12 | | |

4. What is the fourth month of the year? ⬚

5. What time is 1 hour before 4 o' clock?
    ⬚ o' clock

6. 3 is a quarter of ⬚

7. Find the cost of the three toys. ⬚

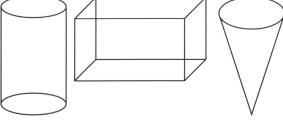

20c   6c   8c

8. 12 is ⬚ less than 15.

9. Colour the cuboid green.

10. $\frac{1}{2}$ a metre and $\frac{1}{2}$ a metre make ⬚ metre.

Score

Practise!

1. How much money in each piggy bank?

┌─────────┐   ┌─────────┐   ┌─────────┐
│   c │   │   c │   │   c │
└─────────┘   └─────────┘   └─────────┘

2. What coins would you use to make the following?

a) 26c = 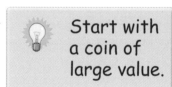 + ⬤ + ⬤

b) 31c = ◯ + ◯ + ◯

> 💡 Start with a coin of large value.

c) 47c = ◯ + ◯ + ◯ + ◯

d) 58c = ◯ + ◯ + ◯ + ◯

e) 86c = ◯ + ◯ + ◯ + ◯ + ◯

f) 93c = ◯ + ◯ + ◯ + ◯ + ◯

3. Name the coin.

a) I am a small brown coin. I am more
   than 1c and less than 5c. What am I? ☐ c

b) I am a gold coin. I am more than 20c. What am I? ☐ c

c) I am equal to 30c – 10c. What am I? ☐ c

d) I am a large gold coin. Two 20c coins and one
   10c coin are the same amount as me. What am I? ☐ c

Mental Maths 15

1. Insert the correct sign < or > or =

   $9 + 3$ ☐ $5 + 6$

2. Colour half the fish green.

3. 20, 16, 12, ☐ , ☐

4. How many months in a year? ☐

5. Is a pencil heavier or lighter than 1 kg?

    ☐

6. What number comes before 70? ☐

7.

   How much money altogether? ☐

8. $14 + 8 +$ ☐ $= 30$

9. $34 + 25 = 30 +$ ☐ $+ 4 + 5$

10. Colour the bottle that holds more.

Practise!

1. How many? cubes ☐ cuboids ☐ spheres ☐
   cylinders ☐ cones ☐

2. True or False? ✓ or ✗.

cube A cube has 6 faces ☐	cuboid A cuboid is a 2-D shape ☐
A cube has 8 corners ☐	A cuboid has 12 sides ☐
A cube has 14 sides ☐	A cuboid has 8 corners ☐
A cube can stack and slide ☐	A cuboid can roll ☐
cylinder A cylinder has 4 faces ☐	sphere A sphere has 1 curved face ☐
A cylinder has 2 edges ☐	A sphere can slide and stack ☐
A cylinder can slide and roll ☐	A sphere has no corners ☐
All the faces of a cylinder are flat ☐	A rugby ball is a sphere ☐

3. The best shape! Pick the best shape for the job.

shoe box ☐   beach ball ☐

wheel ☐   roof of a house ☐

building ☐   flag pole ☐

What's the Shape? Tick ✓ the correct box.

1. This stool is: a sphere ☐ a cube ☐ a cone ☐	2. This box is: a cuboid ☐ a cylinder ☐ a cone ☐

3. A can is: a sphere ☐ a cube ☐ a cylinder ☐	4. This hat is: a cube ☐ a cone ☐ a cylinder ☐	5. An orange is: a cone ☐ a cuboid ☐ a sphere ☐

What am I?

	What am I?	Draw me!
6. I am a 3-D shape that is round. I have no corners. I can roll. I have no straight sides.		
7. I have 6 flat faces. I have 12 straight sides. All my sides are the same length.		
8. I have one curved face and one flat face. My flat face is a circle. I roll around in a circle.		
9. I have 6 faces and 8 corners. Not all my 12 sides are the same. My shape is good for building.		
10. I have 3 faces. My flat faces are circles. I can roll, slide and stack.		

Mental Maths 16

1. One hundred and eighty nine = ☐

2. Colour a quarter of the hearts.

3. John had 17 marbles. He gave 4 to Sarah. He lost 5. How many had he left? ☐

4. The bus left at 4 o'clock. Peter got home at $\frac{1}{2}$ past 4. How long was Peter on the bus? ☐

5. The amount of water in a bottle is measured in a) kilograms or b) litres? ☐

6. Put in the correct sign, < or > or =

    $18 - 6$ ☐ $6 + 5$

7. Colour the tallest tree green.

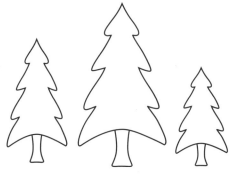

8. How many minutes in 1 hour? ☐ minutes

9.
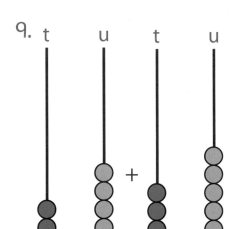

t u t u

\+   \+ $24 + 35 =$ ☐

10. Write the missing number.

+	32	33	34
12	44	45	46
13	45		47
14	46	47	48

Score ☐

Word Problems: At the Seaside

Work it out here:

1. Tom picked 27 shells and Sally picked 25 shells.

    How many did they pick altogether?

    ☐ + ☐ = ☐

t	u

2. An octopus has 8 legs. Jenny saw three octopuses swimming in the sea. How many legs did they have altogether?

    ☐ + ☐ + ☐ = ☐

t	u

3. Anna counted all the boats sailing by the lighthouse. She counted 34 on Saturday and 29 on Sunday. How many boats sailed by the lighthouse?

    ☐ + ☐ = ☐

t	u

4. Sam built 12 sandcastles, Yasmin built 23 and Tanya built 13. How many sandcastles did they build altogether?

    ☐ + ☐ + ☐ = ☐

t	u

5. Granddad swam 21 times in July. He swam 29 times in August. How often did he swim in the sea?

    ☐ + ☐ = ☐

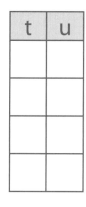

t	u

Test Yourself!

1. 15 + 3 = ☐   13 + 4 = ☐   2. 16 + 2 = ☐   15 + 4 = ☐

3. 11 + 5 = ☐   17 + 2 = ☐   4. 7 + 13 = ☐   10 + 6 = ☐

5.
```
  t u      t u      t u      t u
  4 5      2 1      3 4      1 6
+ 2 4    + 5 4    + 3 5    + 8 3
-----    -----    -----    -----

-----    -----    -----    -----
```

6.
```
  t u      t u      t u      t u
  3 5      1 9      2 7      1 6
+ 4 6    + 5 4    + 3 5    + 6 6
-----    -----    -----    -----

-----    -----    -----    -----
```

7. Dan has 32 cows in a field.
   He has 27 cows in a shed.
   How many cows has Dan altogether?

   ☐ + ☐ = ☐

t	u

8. There are 27 grey donkeys.
   There are 14 brown donkeys.
   How many donkeys live on the farm?

   ☐ + ☐ = ☐

t	u

9. 17 sheep were shorn on Thursday.
   27 were shorn on Friday.
   How many sheep were shorn in total?

   ☐ + ☐ = ☐

t	u

10. Tim has 28 pigs. His Dad has 14.
    Tim buys 18 more pigs.
    How many pigs altogether?

    ☐ + ☐ + ☐ = ☐

t	u

Mental Maths 17

1. How many 20c coins in 1 euro? ☐

2. I am a 2-D shape. I have 3 sides.

   I am a ☐

3. 1 metre = ☐ cm

4. There were 28 pears in a box. 9 were bad.

   How many were good? ☐

5. On the farm there were 12 horses,

   15 pigs and 8 cows.

   How many animals

   altogether? ☐

6. Fill in the missing numbers:

   5, 10, ☐ , 20, ☐

7. €2 =  ◯

8. How many seasons are there in a year? ☐

9. $12 + 3 +$ ☐ $= 30$

10. A bag of carrots weighs $\frac{1}{4}$ kg.

    What is the total weight of

    four bags of carrots? ☐ kg

    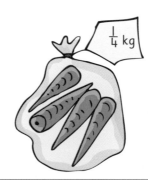

1.
t u	t u	t u	t u	t u	t u
³4̶ ¹1	5 7	7 3	6 1	8 2	5 0
− 1 8	− 2 8	− 5	− 3 4	− 5 5	− 3 2

2.
t u	t u	t u	t u	t u	t u
3 2	4 3	2 3	5 6	7 1	6 4
− 1 5	− 3 4	− 1 9	− 2 7	− 3	− 2 8

3.
t u	t u	t u	t u	t u	t u
³4̶ ¹5	3 6	2 8	6 3	4 8	5 7
− 1 7	− 1 8	− 1 9	− 1 4	− 1 9	− 1 8

4.
t u	t u	t u	t u	t u	t u
5 6	7 3	8 2	4 6	3 7	4 8
− 2 7	− 3 6	− 3	− 2 8	− 2 8	− 3 9

5.
t u	t u	t u	t u	t u	t u
5 9	8 4	5 7	6 4	9 0	8 6
− 2 7	− 1 7	− 5	− 5 3	− 7 7	− 6 4

6. There were 34 cans of dog food on the shelf.
16 were sold on Saturday. How many were left? ☐

7. A shopkeeper had 40 maths copies. 29 copies were bought
by a teacher. How many copies has the shopkeeper now? ☐

1.
```
  t u        t u        t u
  5 2        4 6        6 4
- 1 6      - 1 8      - 3 6
_____    _____    _____
```

2.
```
  t u        t u        t u
  5 3        7 1        6 0
- 2 8      - 5 9      -   5
_____    _____    _____
```

3.
```
  t u        t u        t u
  2 4        6 0        4 5
-   8      - 1 9      - 3 7
_____    _____    _____
```

4.
```
  t u        t u        t u
  4 6        5 2        9 8
- 1 6      - 1 7      - 4 6
_____    _____    _____
```

5.
```
  t u        t u        t u
  6 0        5 6        3 7
- 1 7      - 2 3      - 1 4
_____    _____    _____
```

6.
```
  t u        t u        t u
  2 8        5 0        4 8
- 1 9      -   7      - 2 9
_____    _____    _____
```

7. 48 – 25 = ☐   69 – 23 = ☐   50 – 35 = ☐

8. Joan had 38 stickers. She gave 16 to
   her friend.
   How many has she left? ☐

9. Matt baked 43 buns.
   He sold 24.
   How many has he now? ☐

10. There are 26 horses and 32 cows at the market. How many
    fewer horses than cows are there? ☐

Practise!

1. 34 = ☐ tens and ☐ units   58 = ☐ tens and ☐ units

   14 = ☐ ten and ☐ units   97 = ☐ tens and ☐ units

   28 = ☐ tens and ☐ units   5 = ☐ tens and ☐ units

2. 1 ten and 9 units = ☐   6 tens and 2 units = ☐

   4 tens and 3 units = ☐   8 tens and 1 unit = ☐

   5 tens and 9 units = ☐   7 tens and 5 units = ☐

3. Write the number.

hundreds	tens	units	number

4. Circle the tens.   126   74   108   195   80

5. Circle the units.   117   35   120   4   51

6. Rename: 4 tens and 15 units = ☐ tens and 5 units

   2 tens and 17 units = ☐ tens and ☐ units

   1 ten and 14 units = ☐ tens and ☐ units

Cracking Maths Practice Book – 2nd Class   49

1. What number is shown on the abacus?

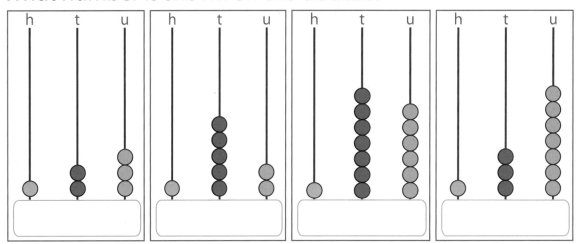

2. Show the number on the abacus.

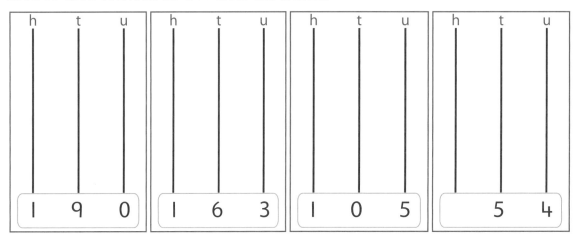

3. 47 = ☐ tens and ☐ units

4. 54 = ☐ tens and ☐ units

5. 5 tens and 6 units = ☐   6. 8 tens and 3 units = ☐

7. 1 ten and 13 units = ☐   8. 2 tens and 17 units = ☐

9. 49 = 4 tens 9 units or 3 tens ☐ units

10. 61 = 6 tens ☐ unit or ☐ tens ☐ units

This is a 100-square numbered from 101 to 200.

101	102			105	106	▲		109	110
111		🦋					118		120
	122			●		127	128		130
131	132	133		135				139	140
♥			144		🦋	🦋		149	150
	152			155					
		163	★		166	167			⬭
	172			175	176		178	179	
181	🦋					187			190
	192		194		197	198	🦋	200	

1. What numbers are hidden under the shapes?

▲ [ ]   ● [ ]   ♥ [ ]   ★ [ ]   ⬭ [ ]

2. What colour are the butterflies over these numbers? Colour the butterflies.

113 =   199 =   182 =   157 =   146 =

3. What numbers come **before** and **after** these numbers?

| | 135 | | | | 159 | | | | 142 | |

| | 184 | | | | 116 | | | | 123 | |

4. What number comes **between** these numbers?

| 102 | | 104 | | 194 | | 196 | | 146 | | 148 |

1. Fill in the missing numbers.

1	2	3		5	6		8	9	10
11	12		14		16	17		19	20
	22	23	24	25		27	28		30
31			34	35	36	37	38	39	
41	42	43			46		48		50
51	52		54	55		57		59	60
61	62	63	64			67	68		
	72	73		75	76			79	80
81		83	84	85		87	88	89	90
91	92			95	96			99	100

2. Match:

10	fifty
20	thirty
30	ten
40	twenty
50	forty
60	eighty
70	seventy
80	sixty
90	one hundred
100	ninety

What comes next or before?

3. 39, 40, 41, ☐ , ☐

4. 72, 73, 74, ☐ , ☐

5. ☐ , ☐ , 35, 36, 37

6. ☐ , ☐ , 63, 64, 65

Write the word **before** or **after**.

7. 16 is ☐ 17   35 is ☐ 36   65 is ☐ 64

8. 80 is ☐ 81   50 is ☐ 49   99 is ☐ 100

9. Match the balloon to the correct word.

twenty-three   fifty-seven   eighty-nine   ninety-four

10. Write in words.

78 = ☐   65 = ☐

Practise!

Area

1. Use the squared paper to colour shapes.
   a) Colour shapes with an area of 3 squares red.
   b) Colour shapes with an area of 4 squares blue.
   c) Colour shapes with an area of 5 squares green.
   d) Colour shapes with an area of 6 squares yellow.
   Some have been done for you. How many more can you find?
   Try to colour shapes in lots of different ways.

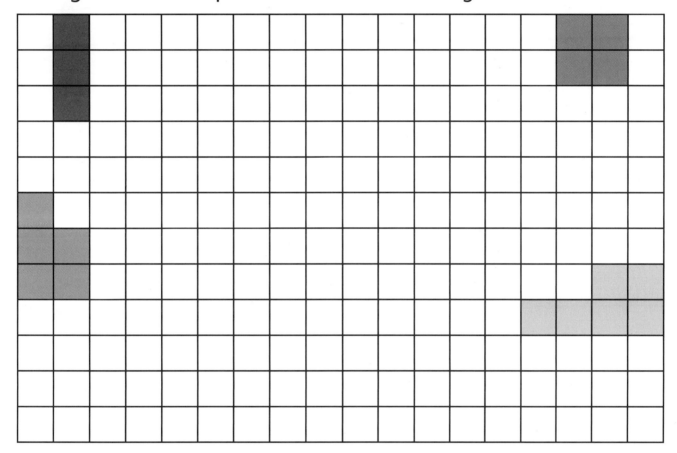

2. What is the area of these shapes in squares?

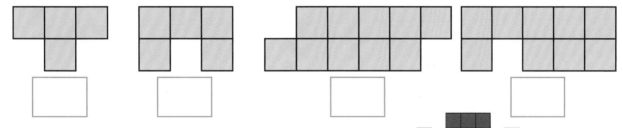

Art Idea!

Create a mosaic using coloured squares.
Discuss the total area covered with your friend.

Mental Maths 18

1. Put these numbers in order, starting with the smallest.

    47   21   76   [ ] [ ] [ ]

2. Name 4 coins you can use to make 36c.

3. Fill in the missing number. 6, 12, 18, [ ] , 30

4. $34 - 16 =$ [ ]

5. Colour $\frac{1}{4}$ of the butterflies.

    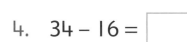

6. A die is in the shape of a [   ]

7. Charlie had 32c. He bought 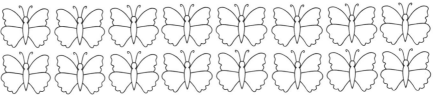 2 pencils. How much had he left? [ ]

8. 10 less than 75 = [ ]

9. [ ] $- 3 = 19$

10. Jim had 20 markers. He lost $\frac{1}{4}$ of them.
    How many has he left? [ ]

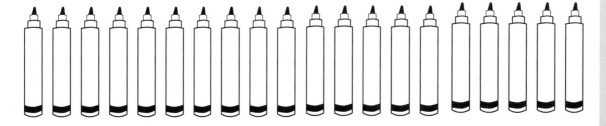

Score

1. Estimate the capacity of the containers in the table.

container	holds less than a litre	holds about a litre	holds more than a litre

2. True ✓ or false ✗ ?

   a) A teapot holds more than $\frac{1}{4}$l.

   b) A kettle holds less than $\frac{1}{2}$l.

   c) A glass holds more than a litre.

   d) A flask holds about $\frac{1}{2}$l.

   e) A can of paint holds more than $\frac{1}{2}$l.

   f) $\frac{1}{2}$l + $\frac{1}{2}$l = 1l

   g) $\frac{1}{4}$l + $\frac{1}{4}$l + $\frac{1}{4}$l = 1l

3. How many bottles of water do I need to make 1 litre?

Water
$\frac{1}{4}$ l

4. A bottle of orange holds $\frac{1}{2}$l. How much would 4 bottles hold?

Orange
$\frac{1}{2}$l

1. Draw two non-standard measuring units that you would use to measure capacity.

2. If you had to measure the capacity of a large basin, which would be better to use, a teaspoon or a cup?

3. Which holds more, a cup or a teapot?

4. Draw a container that holds less than 1 litre.	5. Draw a container that holds more than 1 litre.

6. Mary has a jug that holds 1 litre, 2 mugs that hold $\frac{1}{2}$ litre each, and a kettle that holds 2 litres. How much do they hold altogether?

7. A cup holds $\frac{1}{4}$ litre. A jug holds 1 litre. How many cups are needed to fill the jug?

8. If a basin holds 3 litres and a mug holds $\frac{1}{2}$ litre, how many mugs will it take to fill the basin?

9. A water barrel holds 20l. A can of paint holds 10l. How many litres in 2 barrels and 3 cans ?

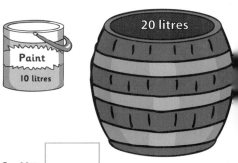

10. A watering can holds 16 litres when full. How many litres does it hold when it is $\frac{1}{2}$ full?

Mental Maths 19

1. There are 29 children in second class. 14 are girls. How many are boys? ▢

2. September is in the season of ▢

3. $143 = $ ▢ hundred, ▢ tens and ▢ units.

4. 25 less than $100 = $ ▢

5. This clock is 2 hours slow. What is the correct time? ▢ | 11:00 |

6. $(8 + 8 + 4) = (15 + $ ▢ $)$

7. Áine is 17. Jane is 5 years younger. How old is Jane? ▢

8. △ Is this shape symmetrical? ▢

9. ▢ $- 4 = 15$

10. Fill in the missing numerals.

165		
	176	
		187

Look at Dad's receipt and answer the questions below.

Mandy's Mini Market

Apples 3@10c	€0.30
Newspaper	€1.20
Cheese	€0.50
Milk	€1.00
Flowers	€1.50
Butter	€0.85
Bread	€0.80
Ham slices	€2.00
Sugar	€0.80
Ice cream	€1.20
Orange juice	€0.50
Bananas 3@15c	€0.45
Carrots	€0.40
Water	€0.50
Total	**€12.00**
Cash	€20.00
Change	€08.00

Thank you for shopping at Mandy's Mini Market
27/6/14   03.15 Lisa

1. What did each of these cost?

   a newspaper ☐   butter ☐

   ice cream ☐   milk ☐

   flowers ☐   bread ☐

   cheese ☐   sugar ☐

2. How much did 3 apples cost? ☐

3. How much would 6 apples cost? ☐

4. How much did 1 banana cost? ☐

5. If Dad only bought bread and milk, what would the total be? ☐

6. What was the cheapest item on the receipt? ☐

7. What would be the cost of the water, carrots and sugar? ☐

8. How much money did Dad spend? ☐

9. What would be the total if Dad didn't buy ham? ☐

10. Find the change from €2.00   Use the euro sign.

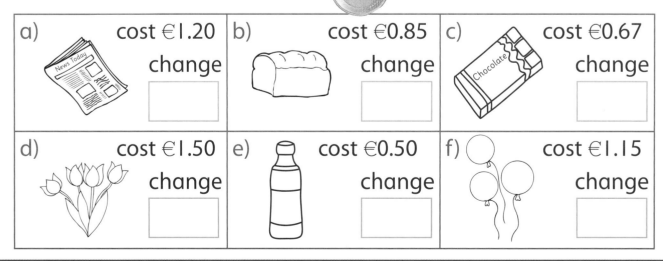

a)	cost €1.20 change ☐	b)	cost €0.85 change ☐	c)	cost €0.67 change ☐
d)	cost €1.50 change ☐	e)	cost €0.50 change ☐	f)	cost €1.15 change ☐

1. How much money in each box?

Draw the correct coins.

2. 49c	3. €1.66

Find the total cost.

4.
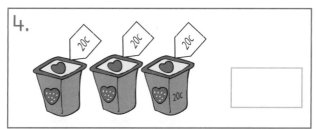
20c 20c 20c 20c

5.
45c Water   €1 Milk   30c

6. Get change from €2.00.

cost	total change
€1.93	c
€1.47	c

7. How many cents?

   a) €1.15 = [   ] c

   b) €0.12 = [   ] c

   c) €0.03 = [   ] c

9. Lisa bought an orange for
   27c and a banana for 30c.
   How much did she spend
   altogether? [   ] c

8. Write using the € sign.

   a) 137c = € [   ]

   b) 68c = € [   ]

   c) 5c = € [   ]

27c
30c

10. What change did Lisa
   get from €2.00? € [   ]

Mental Maths 20

1. How many months are there in half a year? ☐

2. There were 16 oranges in a bag. $\frac{1}{4}$ of them were bad. How many can be eaten? ☐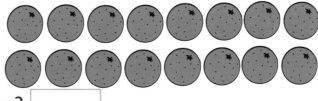

3. A cylinder has 6 faces – true or false? ☐

4. What is the total length of these two pencils? ☐ cm

    14cm

    18cm

5. Fill in the missing numbers.

    ☐ , ☐ , 58 , ☐ , 60

6. There are ☐ fingers altogether.

7. What is the total weight of these items? ☐

    $\frac{1}{4}$ kg   1 kg   Sugar $\frac{1}{4}$ kg

    $\frac{1}{2}$ kg

8. $(3 + 9 + 9) = (15 + $ ☐ $)$

9. 6 is $\frac{1}{4}$ of ☐

10. Fiona has 48 balloons. Ellen has 20 fewer than that. How many balloons have they altogether? ☐

Score

Practise! Two-Step Problem Solving

Read the story and write the number sentence.
Do the part in the brackets first.

1. There are 33 chairs in the classroom.
    The principal took 14 to the hall.
    Later she brought 17 chairs back.
    How many chairs are in the class now?

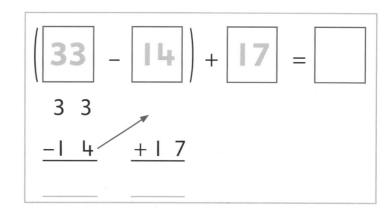

$$\left(\boxed{33} - \boxed{14}\right) + \boxed{17} = \boxed{}$$

```
  3 3
– 1 4      + 1 7
_____      _____
```

2. There were 36 hula hoops.
    14 hoops were broken.
    Miss Brown bought 28 new hoops.
    How many hoops have the children now?

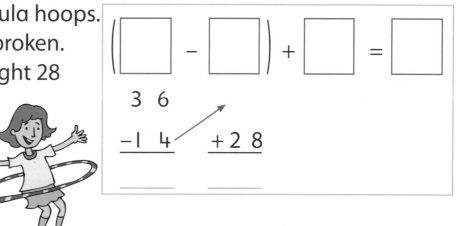

$$\left(\boxed{} - \boxed{}\right) + \boxed{} = \boxed{}$$

```
  3 6
– 1 4      + 2 8
_____      _____
```

3. This time, you choose whether to add or subtract. Put in the **+** or **–** sign.

    Kate won 67 points on a computer game on Monday.
    She lost 29 points on Tuesday.
    On Wednesday Kate scored 38 points.
    How many points did Kate score?

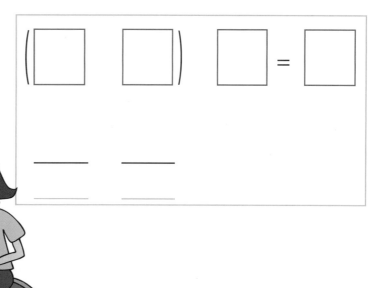

$$\left(\boxed{} \ \boxed{}\right) \ \boxed{} = \boxed{}$$

Test Yourself!

Two-Step Problem Solving

1. (66 + 6) – 48 =

t	u		t	u
6	6			
+	6	–	4	8

2. (72 + 4) – 28 =

t	u		t	u
7	2			
+	4	–	2	8

3. (54 + 17) – 25 =

t	u		t	u

4. (87 – 66) + 24 =

t	u		t	u
–		+		

5. (65 – 24) + 18 =

t	u		t	u
–		+		

6. (72 – 31) + 23 =

t	u		t	u
–		+		

7. (69 – 41) + 51 =

t	u		t	u

8. (35 + 6) + 12 =

t	u		t	u

9. (72 – 34) – 19 =

t	u		t	u

10. Jim has 34 lollipop sticks. His friend Pat has 47 lollipop sticks. They give 28 to Sam. How many lollipop sticks have they left?

(☐ ☐) ☐ = ☐

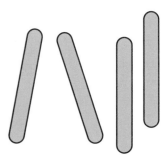